Kerry Hyndman is an illustrator who loves making pictures that spark a sense of wonder in the natural world. She works on a variety of publishing, editorial and advertising projects and has a growing number of non-fiction children's books under her belt. She's also the proud owner of a Blue Peter Book Award (and badge!).

Mike Hills is a writer and journalist who likes to deliver the facts, but have some fun along the way. He has worked for *The Times* and the BBC as a news journalist but increasingly enjoys stepping into the more cheerful world of children's books. He hasn't won any awards (or badges) yet, but he'd like to one day.

The couple live on the west coast of Scotland with their daughter. They like exploring islands, lochs and mountains, finding fairy bridges and waterfalls, falling off paddle boards, swimming with seals and trying to hide from midges.

For Ivy,
Thanks for constantly inspiring us to learn more about this amazing world
of ours and for always asking the best questions about it!

This edition first published in the UK in 2024
This edition first published in the US in 2024
by Faber and Faber Limited
The Bindery, 51 Hatton Garden
London, EC1N 8HN
faber.co.uk

Designed by Clair Lansley
Printed in India

A CIP record for this book is available from the British Library

ISBN 978-0-571-37259-1

MIX
Paper from
responsible sources
FSC® C016779
FSC
www.fsc.org

Printed and bound on FSC® paper in line with our continuing commitment
to ethical business practices, sustainability and the environment.
For further information see faber.co.uk/environmental-policy

2 4 6 8 10 9 7 5 3 1

NATURE'S FASCINATING FRIENDSHIPS

faber

Kerry Hyndman &
Mike Hills

CONTENTS

GETTING BY WITH A LITTLE HELP FROM OUR FRIENDS

There are millions of living things on our incredible planet – so many, in fact, that scientists think we've identified less than a quarter of them!

Most of them go it alone, working among themselves to stay alive and try to thrive. But did you know that some of them join forces and work together?

From crabs who wear sea anemones like boxing gloves to tarantulas with pet frogs, there are lots of examples of species that work and live together to make life a little easier and sometimes more fun! When they do, it's called symbiosis.

So what is symbiosis?

Symbiosis is the scientific term used to describe interactions between different species.

These interactions happen in lots of different ways, and some can annoy or even harm one of the species involved. But we're going to focus on the ones where both sides benefit.

The scientific term for this is mutualistic symbiosis.

Examples of this mutualism have been found at the bottom of the ocean, at the top of mountains, and everywhere in between – and these relationships are often key to the survival of the species involved and their ecosystems. So this book is all about the survival of the friendliest, not the fittest, and we hope it will inspire you to form your own surprising partnerships.

Species are groups of animals, plants and other living organisms that have some similarities and can breed with one another.

These are the two other types of symbiosis: **commensalism** – when one side benefits while the other finds it neither good nor bad; and **parasitism** – when one side harms the other.

But, before we go zooming round the world, we thought we'd introduce you to symbiosis using an example that's a little closer to home . . .

A FRIEND ON THE INSIDE
HUMANS AND BACTERIA

The bacteria in your gut produces 90 per cent of your serotonin, a chemical that plays an important role in whether you feel happy or sad or somewhere in the middle.

Some people try to get more good bacteria in their body by eating certain foods. Can you guess which of these is a popular bacteria booster?
a) sausages
b) chocolate
c) yogurt

?

Every second of every day your body is working hard to keep you healthy, even if you don't notice it. But a lot of this work couldn't be done without a secret helper: bacteria!

It's a little weird to think about, but your body contains TRILLIONS of tiny life forms called microbes, with the majority of them living in parts of your digestive system like the intestines.

Most of the microbes inside you are bacteria that do important jobs like breaking down your food to help you digest it and protecting against germs that could make you sick.

Because this good bacteria has grown up with you, it's learnt how to communicate with your body and explain that it's your friend, not your enemy.

This means that your body allows it to set up home inside you and rewards it with a regular supply of food, while any bad bacteria is kicked out as quickly as possible.

Bacteria was discovered about 350 years ago by a Dutch man called Antonie van Leeuwenhoek, who used a home-made microscope to spot the tiny creatures.

ANSWER – c!

ARCTIC CIRCLE

PACIFIC
OCEAN

ATLANTIC
OCEAN

EQUA

NORTH AMERICA

This continent is mostly made up of the United States of America, Mexico, Canada and Greenland – so it stretches from just north of the equator all the way to the Arctic Circle.

That means you can find everything from sweaty swamps and desperately dry deserts to glaciers and snow-capped mountains.

Some of the most notable animals that live in North America are black bears, polar bears, bald eagles, racoons and alligators.

Can you see any rival predators that the raven should warn the wolf about? They're often found lurking in the bushes . . .

Ravens are super clever. Experiments have found that their problem-solving skills are often more advanced than those of young children – especially when food's involved.

HEY, PAL, OVER HERE!

RAVENS AND WOLVES

Every hunter could do with a little help from a friend, especially one that can see everything from above. For wolves, that help comes in the feathered form of a raven. If the big black bird spots animal carcasses that look too tough for it to peck through itself, it calls its pal.

When wolves hear that distinctive caw, they know it's dinner time – and their clever friend leads them straight to the food. The raven stays alert and keeps an eye out for any trouble (like a hungry bear) while the wolves enjoy their meal. If all goes well, the raven gets the leftovers.

Like all partnerships, they have their ups and downs, and the scavenging birds have been known to take more than their fair share of a carcass. In fact, some experts think one of the reasons wolves hunt in a pack is to stop their cheeky chums from stealing all the food.

BOXING BUDDIES

LYBIA CRABS AND SEA ANEMONES

If an anemone is dropped or snatched away, the crab simply breaks its remaining one in two, and – incredibly – both parts are able to regenerate and continue stinging.

Lybia crabs are about the same size as a small coin and spend most of their time wandering the ocean floor. Being such a small creature makes them vulnerable to bigger sea-roaming predators – but if they don't look worried it's because they have a secret weapon.

Get too close and you'll find out why they're also known as boxer crabs. One jab from them can cause a mighty pain thanks to the stinging tentacles of the beautiful sea anemones that they carry with them in each claw like boxing gloves.

The protection of the anemones is so important to the crabs that they can get quite controlling over their little friends, restricting food and sometimes munching away at them to ensure they don't get too big to carry around.

It may seem like a one-way relationship, but being moved about by the crabs does help the anemones gather more food than they could do by themselves.

Badgers have been known to bury animal carcasses that are too big for them to eat in one sitting. Researchers in the US filmed one burying an animal in a desert that was much bigger than a badger – but what was it?
a) kangaroo
b) cow
c) coyote

?

A-HUNTING WE WILL GO
COYOTES AND BADGERS

This peculiar pair certainly supports the idea that opposites attract. Coyotes have a reputation for being fast and cunning while badgers are often seen as slow and clumsy. But, on the grasslands of North America, they've formed the perfect partnership.

Despite their differences, the two animals share a love for rodents like mice and voles, and they've learnt that hunting together makes their lives much easier.

Coyotes, with their super sense of smell, are brilliant at finding and chasing their prey, while badgers, who trundle along behind, can use their strong, sharp claws to easily uncover underground dens if their victim tries to tunnel to safety.

The thrill of the chase can get a bit much for the badgers, though, so in the winter months they go it alone and take a slower approach to filling their stomachs – rummaging around underground and scooping out hibernating rodents at their own pace.

This cute couple may just be one of the oldest recorded examples of co-operating animals, with stories of their endeavours written into Native American folklore.

ANSWER - b)

21

The moths are a tasty meal for birds and bats, but because they're the same whitish colour as the yucca plant's flowers they can use that camouflage to stay safe. There are six yucca moths in this scene, but can you find them all?

?

The yucca moth and the yucca plant have been buddies for millions of years now, and there's a good reason for their friendship – neither of them would survive without the other!

Their incredible relationship is based on an unspoken agreement between the two species: the moths act as the plant's only pollinator, ensuring that more yuccas can grow, while the moths get the perfect little place to lay their precious eggs in return.

Plants grow from seeds, and those seeds are made through the process of pollination. This happens when a powdery substance called pollen is transferred from the male part of a plant (a stamen) to the female part (a carpel).

To ensure their babies have enough food to go around, the moths release chemicals into the air (called pheromones) to warn off other moths and stop overcrowding.

When a female moth is ready to deposit her eggs, she first gathers pollen from other plants and carefully carries it under her chin to her chosen yucca plant. There she makes a tiny hole in the plant for her eggs, before placing the pollen on the stigma.

This pollinates the flower and means that, when the moth's babies hatch, they have enough yummy yucca seeds to feast on, which is the only thing the insects eat. Magic!

STAMEN

CARPEL

A FLOWERING FRIENDSHIP

YUCCA MOTHS AND YUCCA PLANTS

The Clark's nutcracker might look like another unassuming member of the crow family, but it's actually a pretty amazing bird that helps define an entire ecosystem.

They like to eat the tasty seeds inside a whitebark pine tree's cone, so they go from branch to branch, using their long, strong beaks to collect them. A pouch under their tongue can store between 50 and 150 seeds, and when that's full they head to the ground to bury them.

In the winter, when they get hungry, they use their amazing memory to retrace their movements and find the buried treasure.

Nutcrackers are thought to collect up to 100,000 seeds every year – with one study suggesting they can gather about 30 seeds a minute if they're in a rush!

But they always store more than they need, so the remaining seeds eventually become fully grown whitebark pines and keep the cycle going.

Lots of other animals eat these seeds – which are also known as pine nuts – like squirrels, chipmunks and even grizzly bears! But the nutcrackers are the only ones who help new trees grow by burying the seeds in soil, a process the trees rely on to continue reproducing.

TREASURE HUNTERS
CLARK'S NUTCRACKERS AND WHITEBARK PINE TREES

Each nutcracker stores its seeds in lots of different locations, and scientists think the birds memorise key objects to help them locate their food. Can you find the spot where this nutcracker buried its stash? It's between a large tree and a stream.

The Clark's nutcracker gets its name from William Clark, an American explorer who spotted the bird during an expedition to uncharted land in the US in 1805.

SNOT ATTACK!
UPSIDE-DOWN JELLYFISH AND ALGAE

As the name suggests, the upside-down jellyfish isn't an ordinary jellyfish. Instead of gliding elegantly through the water, this one prefers to chill on the seabed and soak up some rays.

The reason it does this is because it gets its energy from its housemate: algae! This organism lives inside the arms of the jellyfish and is photosynthetic, which means it can capture sunlight and carbon dioxide and create natural sugars (food!) in the process.

To ensure the algae can take in as much sunlight as possible, these jellyfish tend to be found in warm, shallow spots lying on their bell (the bit that looks like the top of an umbrella) with their arms spread wide.

The jellyfish are thought to receive as much as 90 per cent of the nutrients they need from the algae, who get a protected habitat in return. For the other 10 per cent, the jellyfish feed on plankton that they stun by firing a snot-like mucus that carries stinging cells out into the water. Yuck!

Plankton aren't the only creatures hit by the flying mucus – humans diving nearby often find themselves covered in irritating, itchy stings when they get out of the water without even touching a jellyfish.

Algae has also been found in these snot-bombs, and scientists believe this might explain why the blobs of mucus keep moving for a long time after being fired. But can you guess how long?
a) 24 hours
b) a week
c) 10 days

?

EUROPE

On a clear, sunny day in southern Spain, you can look out from Europe and see Africa just across the water, but the continent's northernmost point sits in the Arctic Circle. Since the majority of Europe has a mild climate, the biodiversity is less rich than in warmer regions of the world, but it still has a wide variety of plants and animals. Its woods and forests are home to an array of eagles, woodpeckers and owls, and you'll find whales, dolphins and jellyfish in its waters. You might even spot some bears in the east or north.

ARCTIC CIRCLE

ATLANTIC OCEAN

EQUATOR

Our oceans are full of peculiar-looking creatures, but there aren't many that are more peculiar than the sunfish, a giant slab of a creature that likes to gobble up jellyfish.

To find the juiciest jellyfish, sunfish are happy to dive down into the coldest depths of the sea, but once they're full they head back up to the surface and lie on their side for a spot of sunbathing to help warm themselves up.

Unfortunately, on their travels they pick up a lot of parasites – little bugs that like to bite and suck out nutrients from their victims. So, if the sunbathing is interrupted by an itch they can't scratch, they call for help by flapping their fins on the surface of the water.

At the sound of the splash, seagulls suddenly appear and swoop down to lend a beak. The gulls drop their heads into the water and peck off the parasites, meaning they get a decent snack, and the sunfish get a much-needed grooming that stops them from becoming infested.

PECKING FOR PARASITES
SUNFISH AND SEAGULLS

Seagulls aren't the only things sunfish turn to when they want a good scrub – they also let cleaner fish have a nibble and even use floating kelp fields like a car wash.

Baby sunfish are tiny, measuring just 2mm long, but they grow BIG! One sunfish found off the coast of Japan was nearly 3m long, but can you guess how much it weighed?
a) more than a washing machine
b) more than a motorbike
c) more than a large car

?

ANSWER – c! It weighed more than 2,000kg.

These networks can have a dark side too. Some trees, like the black walnut, can send chemicals via the fungal threads that stop its rivals from growing.

If a tree knows that it's dying, it will empty its store of nutrients into the fungal network and share them with other trees before it has completely died.

THE FUNGUS AMONG US
TREES AND FUNGI

When you walk through a forest, trees look like they're competing against one another to see who can grow the tallest and capture the most sunlight. But under your feet there is a magical world that shows that the forest is as much about co-operation as competition.

Just below the ground, the sprawling roots of the trees come alive as they share food and knowledge with each other through a mysterious network of fungi that is referred to as the 'wood-wide web' because of the similarities it shares with the internet.

The trees need this network because the tiny fungal threads are able to reach further into the earth than their own roots and suck up important nutrients. In return for sharing these nutrients, the fungi gets the tasty natural sugars that trees produce.

Researchers have also found that trees use the network to help one another, warning their neighbours if they're being attacked by a disease or insects, or by sending sugars to younger trees to give them a better chance of survival.

Trees are able to recognise the roots of trees that they're related to using the fungi and can direct resources to those relations rather than other unrelated neighbours.

33

If you like nothing more than eating strawberries with your breakfast or biting into a crunchy apple at lunch, remember to say thank you the next time you see a bee buzz by. Without them, there would be far fewer fruits and vegetables in our supermarkets.

This is because bees play a crucial role in lots of ecosystems all over the world by pollinating flowers that often wouldn't be able to reproduce if it wasn't for their bumbling buddies.

Bees pollinate flowers when they stop off to drink the sweet nectar inside and rub against pollen on the stamen. When they fly off to the next flower, they transport and deposit the pollen, which enables the flowers to grow seeds and create more plants.

Plants try their hardest to attract bees because their survival depends on this pollination. They do so by making their petals as brightly coloured as possible and sending out strong, sweet smells that lure the excited insects straight to them.

One reason pollen sticks to bees so readily is because the busy little creatures have a slight electrical charge that's produced by the friction they create when they whizz through the air.

PRO POLLINATORS

FLOWERS AND BEES

Bees use the nectar they gather from plants to make honey. But do you know how much honey one bee makes in its entire lifetime?
a) less than a teaspoon
b) a full jar
c) a full swimming pool

The honeybee has some pretty good moves and performs a special 'waggle' dance when it's found a good food source to direct other bees to it.

ANSWER – a) Most bees only live for a few weeks or months.

35

WHAT'S NOT TO LICHEN?
ALGAE AND FUNGI

Lichens can survive in some of the most extreme conditions, so there are lots of them. In fact, experts think they cover between 5 and 10 per cent of the Earth's surface.

After a natural disaster like a wildfire or a volcanic eruption, lichens are often the first organisms to return because of their ability to grow where nothing else can.

Photosynthesis is the chemical reaction inside plants that uses carbon dioxide, water and light to make oxygen and glucose – a sugary food for the plant.

Lichens are plant-like organisms that grow where plants can't – on rocks near the beach and on trees in the woods, for example. But did you know they wouldn't exist – or be able to survive in those places – without the magical relationship that creates them?

The two organisms that unite to make lichens are fungi and algae. Algae is a very small type of plant, so it's able to create natural sugars through photosynthesis. The fungi needs these sugars to grow, but can't create them on its own, so it offers the algae some structural protection from the weather in return for this food.

On the inside, most lichens are generally very similar, but on the outside they can come in all sorts of weird and wonderful shapes and sizes. Scientists now believe that some of these physical differences may be because of another fungal partner in the relationship: yeast.

Lichens are thought to be some of the oldest living organisms on Earth, with one type found in the Arctic estimated to have been there for more than 8,000 years.

A SHORT BUT SWEET LIFE

FIG TREES AND FIG WASPS

The life of a fig wasp is pretty short. It begins and ends inside the fruit of a fig tree – but the tiny creature plays a crucial role in the plant's survival.

Figs are essentially flowers that bloom inside themselves, making it incredibly difficult for them to be pollinated. Thankfully, they've got a special relationship with fig wasps that they've developed over the last 60 million years or so.

With bodies that are just a couple of millimetres in size, these wasps are able to crawl inside tiny gaps in the fruit (losing their wings in the process) and pollinate them with pollen that they've carried from the fig tree they were born in.

Once inside, these female wasps safely deposit their eggs before their short life comes to an end, in an act of motherly sacrifice that guarantees the insects and plants will live on.

Don't worry: when you eat a fig, you won't find any crunchy wasps inside because the fruit will have already digested the insects and turned them into protein – a useful thing to eat because it helps your body grow!

Male fig wasps are wingless and never actually leave the fig. Their only purpose after mating is to dig a tunnel through the fruit for the female wasp to depart.

A GLOW FROM BELOW

LANTERNFISH AND BACTERIA

Lanternfish are pretty small, and most of the 200 or so different types would easily fit in the palm of your hand – but there are A LOT of them. In fact, research suggests they make up more than half of the total biomass of all the deep-sea fish in the world!

You're unlikely to ever see a lanternfish while you're splashing around in the sea, though, because they're usually hundreds of metres below the surface. At that depth, the water gets really dark, and that's where the lanternfish's name starts to make sense.

Their bodies are covered in light-producing organs called photophores, which are able to light up like a lantern thanks to the bioluminescent bacteria inside them, which is more than happy to assist in return for a home and a constant supply of food.

Lanternfish use the lights in different ways, such as turning them on to attract smaller fish at feeding time and also to make their silhouette harder to spot against the lighter water above them when predators are lurking below.

Can you spot another type of fish that can glow thanks to bioluminescent bacteria? And do you know what its name is?

Lanternfish play a key role in fighting climate change because they eat a lot of plankton that is rich in carbon, which would otherwise seep into the atmosphere.

Lanternfish swim around in such dense groups that they're able to reflect sound waves, which can be confusing for scientists who use them to measure how deep the ocean floor is.

ANSWER – It's the creepy-faced anglerfish, of course!

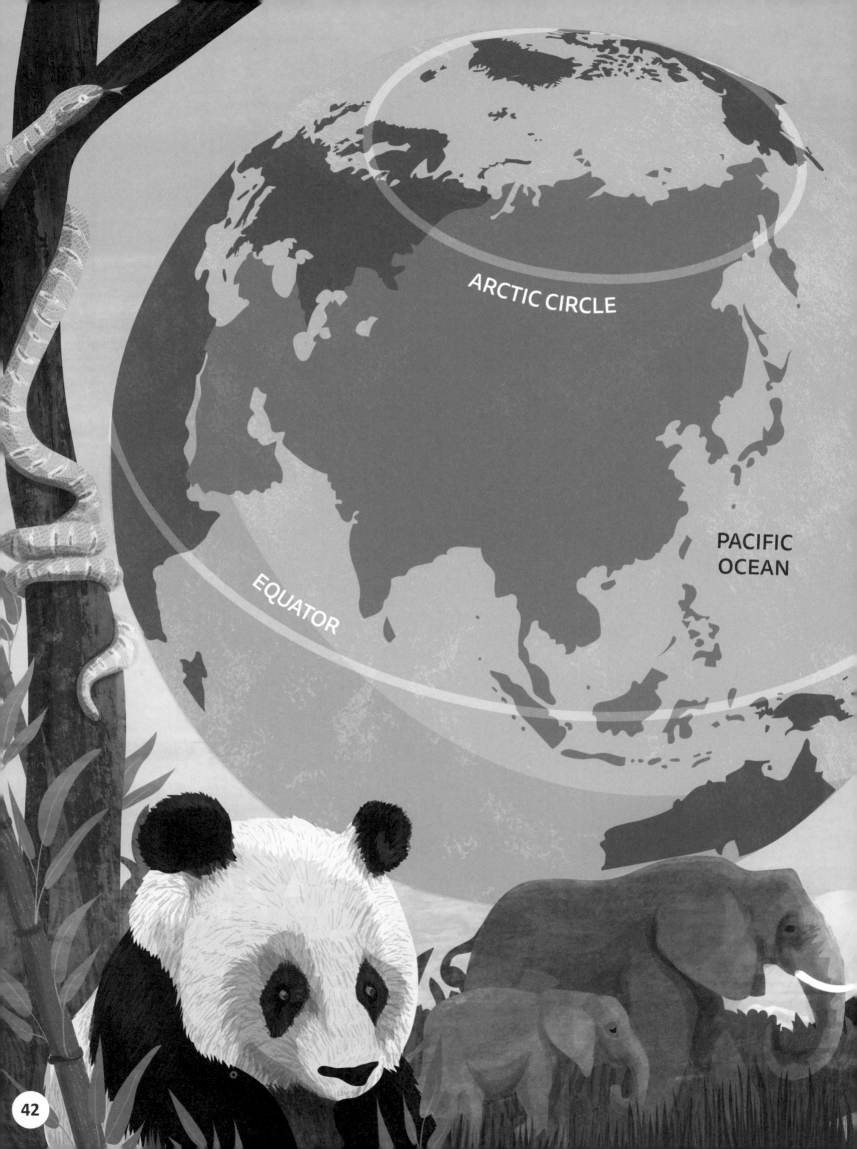

ARCTIC CIRCLE

PACIFIC
OCEAN

EQUATOR

ASIA

Asia is the largest continent, stretching from the Middle East to Japan, and with a population of about 4.7 billion it's where the majority of people on the planet live. The Himalayas mountain range, which sits between India and China, contains the highest peak in the world: Mount Everest. Incredibly, the mountains there get higher every year as the large slabs of rock beneath them – known as tectonic plates – continue to push against one another. Because it covers such a large area, Asia is home to an amazing bunch of animals, including tigers, elephants, pandas, camels and snakes.

The term 'carnivorous' is usually used to describe meat-eating animals, but some plants – like the pitcher plant – are also carnivores and get their nutrients from eating insects and small animals like frogs. Or, of course, poo!

SUCK IT UP, PAL

BATS AND PITCHER PLANTS

This is one of those partnerships that will have you going 'aww' and 'eww' in equal measure.

You might think that bats like to find nice dark caves to get some sleep, but the woolly bat prefers something a little more luxurious. After a busy night of hunting, this creature escapes the sunshine by climbing into a pitcher plant and getting cosy.

The plant isn't just a sleeping bag for the bat, though: it's also a toilet. As it

relieves itself, the plant eagerly sucks up the nutrients carried in the poo – and they are vital to the carnivorous plant's survival since research suggests it's pretty bad at catching insects.

The relationship is so important that both the bat and the plant have evolved to ensure it continues – with the woolly bat's echolocation using a higher pitch to help find the pitcher, and the plant increasing the size of its entrance to make it easier to be found.

Echolocation is a technique animals use to find objects with their ears rather than their eyes. By making a noise and waiting to hear what it bounces off, they can work out where an object is, its direction of travel and size.

Woolly bats aren't the only animals to use pitcher plants as a toilet: mountain tree shrews also relieve themselves while feeding on the plant's sweet nectar.

A BEAUTIFUL STING
CLOWNFISH AND SEA ANEMONES

Clownfish would struggle to survive without the protection of a sea anemone, so this means they never stray too far from home – unlike Nemo!

If you watch a sea anemone eating, you'll see it suck its prey into the top of its body and then fire the waste out of the same hole because its mouth is also its bum!

If there's one symbiotic relationship you knew about before reading this book, it was probably this one! The distinctive markings of a clownfish and the beautiful, bright colours of sea anemones make this a particularly eye-catching partnership.

But the beauty of sea anemones is actually part of their deadly appeal. They use their good looks to lure small fish towards them before zapping them with a powerful sting and gobbling them up. Gulp!

Luckily for clownfish, they're covered in a coat of mucus that protects them from the sea anemone's sting and allows them to glide in among the deadly tentacles and set up home.

This high-security hotel keeps clownfish safe from predators and gives them somewhere secure to lay their eggs. In return, they keep the space nice and clean, and the sea anemones get to feast on the nutritious waste of their room-mates.

Treehoppers can be found on every continent apart from Antarctica, but you've probably not spotted one because they've evolved to blend in with their surroundings.

One member of this insect family has some peculiar headgear that scientists believe helps it imitate a deadly fungus, while another has a thorn-like spike on its head.

While these structures may help them ward off some predators, treehoppers also have a dedicated team of security guards made up of . . . ants!

Why would ants be so protective of another insect? Well, treehoppers spend a lot of their time sucking the juicy sap from plants, and what goes in must come out, so when they release this sugary substance the ants are ready and waiting to drink it up.

As well as providing security, entomologists also think the ants act as farmers by increasing the amount of sap the treehoppers extract through moving them to better locations on the plant. Pretty clever for such a small insect!

An entomologist is someone who studies insects. Observing bugs, bees, butterflies and more has helped humans learn a huge amount about our planet, especially as insects have lived here for at least 400 million years.

Treehoppers are thought to have been around for at least 40 million years, with fossils of the insects found in the Dominican Republic dating that far back.

Some 3,000 different types of treehoppers have been found around the world, all different shapes and sizes. But do you think there are more or fewer species of ants?

TREE-MENDOUS FRIENDS
TREEHOPPERS AND ANTS

ANSWER – There are more – A LOT more! At least 10,000 different types have been found so far.

Sea urchins might look like plants, but they're definitely animals. They have a mouth on the underside of their body and, although they don't have eyes, scientists think they have special light sensors on the end of their spines that allow them to see.

A HAT WITH A POINT

CARRIER CRABS AND SEA URCHINS

There are a surprisingly high number of sea predators who like to crack open a crab for dinner – octopuses, turtles and rays, for example – so crabs have to get a little creative to stay safe.

The carrier crab has five pairs of legs, but only uses the front ones to move about because the back ones are busy carrying its spiny security guard: a sea urchin.

The two species have forged a partnership that sees the crab get some protection from its spiky friend, who is covered in brightly coloured spines, while the urchin lives a life of luxury and gets carried around as it feeds on the crab's scraps.

Sea urchins are lightweight, so they're pretty easy for the crab to carry, especially since their back legs have evolved to have hook-like tips that help them hold on tight to their friend.

Sometimes there's a third creature involved in this relationship as well, with small fish often setting up home among the urchin's spines. How many fish can you spot hanging out in these spines?

ANSWER – There are nine fish!

Marsh frogs are the largest native frog in Europe and also make a very distinctive noise, but can you guess what it sounds like?
a) a car starting
b) someone laughing
c) a toilet flushing

?

FANCY A FROGGYBACK?

WATER BUFFALOES AND MARSH FROGS

This odd partnership was spotted in some wetlands in Turkey by birdwatchers who were surprised to see some tiny frogs sitting on the backs of water buffaloes in the marshes.

Now why would these little amphibians want to hop all the way up there? For nibbles, of course! The frogs like to feast on the insects nestled in the buffalo's coat, providing a useful beauty service to the big beasts and removing some of their parasites.

Researchers believe the frogs only hop aboard their pals in the autumn, possibly because that's when the frog population is at its highest, and there's increased competition for food.

As well as providing a good source of snacks, the body heat of the water buffaloes helps their fly-catching friends warm up when the temperature drops.

While it's not entirely clear if the buffaloes signed up for the deal, they do appear to get something out of it – even if it's just having an itch scratched.

The average number of frogs found riding on the backs of the buffaloes was between 2 and 5 – but one buffalo was seen carrying 27 frogs!

ANSWER – b) Their call sounds like a duck giggling and explains why they're sometimes called 'laughing frogs'.

A MASTER OF DISGUISE
BOBTAIL SQUIDS AND BACTERIA

Bobtail squids are pretty small, usually not much bigger than a button, but they have comparatively big brains, and they use them to great effect to avoid predators.

During the day, they try to keep a low profile by burying themselves in sand on the seabed or by using special cells in their body to change colour and blend in with their surroundings. And, if they're spotted, they can fire a cloud of ink to hide their speedy escape.

But at night, when a squid goes hunting for shrimp and other crustaceans, it turns to the bioluminescent bacteria inside it to help provide some camouflage. The light this bacteria produces allows the squid to blend in with the glow of the moon and stars, stopping big fish below from seeing it.

It's a complex relationship, though, and, while the bacteria gets a room for the night, the squid ejects it in the morning. After a brief break from each other, the squid allows the bacteria to come back again to ensure its superpower is ready for the next night.

Bobtail squids are so good at disguising themselves that the US Air Force has studied them to see if they could learn anything that could improve the camouflage on their aeroplanes.

Let's see how good their camouflage really is. There are eight bobtail squids in this scene, but can you find them all?

SOUTH AMERICA

South America is dominated by Brazil, which covers about half of the continent's land mass and borders nearly every other country within it. The Amazon River, which snakes from the mountains of Peru in the west to the coast of Brazil in the east, supports the largest rainforest in the world and a huge variety of ecosystems. Other important spots for nature include Costa Rica in the north, whose jungles are home to jaguars, monkeys, sloths and toucans, and the Galapagos Islands, which are famous for their giant tortoises, iguanas and penguins.

ATLANTIC
OCEAN

EQUATOR

PACIFIC
OCEAN

ANTARCTIC CIRCLE

57

FRIENDS IN NEED
PASSION FLOWERS AND SWORD-BILLED HUMMINGBIRDS

Have you ever seen a beak as long as that? Probably not, because the sword-billed hummingbird is the only bird in the world with a beak that is longer than its body.

Thanks to the wonders of evolution, its beak has grown to be exactly the right size to reach its favourite snack: the nectar deep inside the passion flower. So, when the bird is feeling hungry, it heads straight for the flower, hovering next to it with its wings flapping so quickly they're just a blur, before dropping its beak in for a slurp of the sweet stuff.

As it flies from one plant to another, it distributes the powdery pollen caught on its beak. This is a really important job as the hummingbird is the passion flower's only pollinator, so the plant would struggle to survive without regular visits from its feathery friend.

Equally, the bird has become so reliant on the flower's nectar that its own future would also be at risk if the plant died out.

Because its beak is so long, the hummingbird can't use it to clean itself, so instead it has to use its feet to brush off any dirt and rearrange its feathers.

Evolution is the idea that all living things change over time to give themselves a better chance of survival. The theory was first put forward by Charles Darwin in the 1800s.

As well as having a super-long beak, the sword-billed hummingbird also has a super-long tongue and, just like the bird's wings, it moves incredibly fast to lap up the nectar as quickly as possible.

pollen

nectar chambers

59

A FISHER'S FRIEND
HUMANS AND
BOTTLENOSE DOLPHINS

Bottlenose dolphins have perfectly streamlined bodies for swimming, and they can hit speeds of over 30 miles per hour in a sprint, but they prefer to trundle along at 3 miles per hour most of the time.

Fishing can often involve a lot of guesswork to uncover the best spot to catch something, but fishers in Brazil have found something that greatly improves their chances: dolphins.

For more than a hundred years, bottlenose dolphins have been helping locals by herding schools of fish towards the shore, where dozens of people wait for the right moment before casting their nets into the water.

No one is sure how this co-operation started, but the fishers say they would catch far fewer fish without the help they get from their finned friends. And they do feel like friends, with the locals recognising the animals' markings and often giving them names.

As for what the dolphins get in return, no one's really sure about that either. But, when the fishing nets hit the water, the fish flee in the opposite direction and straight into the path of the dolphins, meaning they catch their dinner with minimal effort as well.

Those long legs and big ears might look a little peculiar, but they help the maned wolf hunt in long grass and hear even the slightest movement from its prey. Can you spot any prey nearby?

While maned wolves aren't endangered just yet, their numbers are declining. One of the reasons is the destruction of their habitat by humans who want to use the forests for farming and other purposes instead. This is known as deforestation.

PECULIAR PALS AND POWERFUL POO

MANED WOLVES, WOLF APPLES AND LEAFCUTTER ANTS

When the seed of a plant begins to grow, it's called germination – and the process begins when roots and a shoot emerge from the seed.

When is a wolf not a wolf? Well, this animal might share the name, but with a face like a fox and legs like a deer it certainly doesn't look like a wolf – and that's because it's not one!

The maned wolf is so unique that it's the only member of its genus – meaning it shares few similarities with any other animals – and can be found roaming across the swamps, savannahs, grasslands and forests of several South American countries.

It's this roaming that is so important to the symbiotic relationship it has with its favourite snack – the fruit of the lobeira plant, known as a wolf apple.

After chowing down on the fruit, the leggy member of the dog family turns into a super-spreader as it distributes the plant's seeds far and wide in its poo, helping to increase the germination rate.

Some of this poo (and the seeds inside it) often ends up on top of the nests of leafcutter ants. But they don't mind because they bury it and use it as fertiliser for the fungus they grow, which helps produce more lobeira plants and keeps maned wolves fed.

COMING OUT OF MY SHELL

GIANT GALAPAGOS TORTOISES AND FINCHES

Giant Galapagos tortoises are pretty incredible creatures. They might not be very quick, but they have great stamina and can live for over 150 years – longer than any other land animal.

Fully grown, their shells can measure more than one metre across, and they can weigh over 250kg, so you can imagine they're not the most flexible of animals.

That means that when they get an itch somewhere on their giant body, they need to call for some help – and that help comes from a friendly finch.

The tortoise signals for its pal by fully extending its long neck from within its shell. When the bird appears, it hops on to the tortoise and begins pecking away at the parasitic bugs that are causing its friend some discomfort.

When the meal's over, the bird leaves with a tummy full of bugs, and the tortoise can retreat back into its shell with a few less itches to scratch.

The finches in the Galapagos Islands are known as Darwin's finches – named after Charles Darwin, whose visit to the islands in 1835 inspired his theory of evolution.

If these tortoises have a superpower, it's stockpiling. Their amazing ability to store food and water in their bodies means they could survive a year without eating or drinking anything.

A LEAP OF FAITH
TARANTULAS AND FROGS

Like all tarantulas, the Colombian lesserblack does have a venomous bite – but, while it can be fatal for prey like mice, it's not considered very dangerous to humans.

The tarantula is often thought of as a big, scary predator, and the Colombian lesserblack is one of the biggest, with a 7cm-long body and a legspan of around 20cm. But this spider does have a cute side – if you get to know it.

Look carefully when it's prowling and the chances are you'll see a little frog hopping along behind. Now you might assume that the spider would turn, strike and gobble up the little amphibian as soon as it notices it, but you'd be wrong.

The word to describe a person's fear of spiders is arachnophobia, but do you know the word for a fear of frogs?
a) amphibiphobia
b) frognophobia
c) ranidaphobia

?

Toxins are a type of poisonous substance that are naturally produced by some plants and animals, and they can be harmful to other organisms.

The tiny dotted humming frog, which is about as big as your thumb, has toxins in its skin that make it a terrible-tasting snack and may help explain its unlikely friendship with tarantulas.

Not only do the scary spiders offer the frogs protection from predators like snakes, they also invite their four-legged friends to live with them in their underground burrows. Helpfully, the frogs are quick to eat any ants that come looking for spider eggs to feast on.

ANSWER – c) It's ranidaphobia, and it gets its name from the scientific word for the family of frogs – Ranidae.

DON'T CALL ME LAZY!

SLOTHS, MOTHS AND ALGAE

Sloths are thought to have the slowest digestive system of any animal, and it can take them weeks to break down their food.

Sloths have amazing necks, which allow them to turn their heads 270 degrees and nibble leaves all around them without moving the rest of their body.

If you only know one thing about sloths, it's probably that they move v-e-r-y s-l-o-w-l-y. They're one of the most chilled-out mammals on the planet, and their rather relaxed approach to cleanliness has helped create an impressively complex ecosystem within their fur.

Sloths move that slowly not out of laziness but to conserve energy, and the reason they need to is their diet, which is mostly made up of leaves. Thankfully, this slow pace means predators struggle to spot them, but there's something else that helps them stay safe: algae!

The layer of green algae that forms on their fur acts as camouflage, allowing the sloths to blend in with their surroundings as they hang from trees. Lots of other creatures also like exploring this thick fur, although most of them are parasites like mosquitoes and ticks.

Moths, however, have developed an understanding with their furry friends. Sloths only leave the safety of the treetops once a week to go to the toilet – but, when they do, the moths fly out of the fur and lay their eggs in the fresh poo. When the eggs hatch, the larvae live in the poo until they're fully developed and then, once they're ready, they fly up to find a sloth and help their buddies out by fertilising their algae.

ARCTIC CIRCLE

ATLANTIC
OCEAN

EQUATOR

PACIFIC
OCEAN

ANTARCTIC CIRCLE

70

AFRICA

It might be home to the Sahara, the world's largest hot desert, but there's more to Africa than sand. You can find penguins at its southern tip, but the continent is best known for the five big beasts that roam across southern Africa: lions, leopards, elephants, rhinos and buffaloes. The Nile, one of the longest rivers in the world, also supports a wide variety of animals, such as crocodiles, hippos and turtles, and plants like bamboo and banana trees. The tropical forests in sub-Saharan Africa are also where you'll find the world's only wild gorillas.

YOU SCRATCH MY BACK ...

OXPECKERS AND LARGE MAMMALS

Oxpeckers like to keep busy, which is lucky because some of Africa's biggest beasts would be pretty grumpy if they didn't turn up for work. The important job these birds have is removing harmful parasites from large mammals like rhinos, hippos, giraffes and zebras.

So oxpeckers spend their days hopping from one big animal to the next, stiffening their tail feathers for balance and using specially adapted feet to cling on to their giant buddies. Their hosts trust them so much they even let them dig around in their ears for ticks.

African buffalo

Zebra

In return, the birds get all the food they need since parasites, dead skin and earwax are some of their favourite snacks!

The bad news for oxpeckers is that some of their best friends are at risk of becoming extinct. If hunters continue to kill Africa's big beasts, this beautiful bird's future could be in doubt.

As well as using the big beasts for food, oxpeckers also get something else useful from their hosts, but can you guess what?
a) toenails
b) hair
c) poo

?

Giraffe

Greater kudu

ANSWER – b! The oxpeckers gather hair and fur to use for a little extra comfort in their nests.

Oxpeckers help out their rhino buddies in another way too. Rhinos have pretty bad eyesight so, if the bird spots a predator or poacher on the prowl, it sounds the alarm.

Black rhinoceros

73

A SWEET DEAL

GREATER HONEYGUIDES AND HUMANS

Honeyguides are often said to co-operate with honey badgers in the same way that they interact with humans, but sadly there's no real evidence to prove it.

To achieve the magical call that summons the honeyguides, some people whistle, using a hollowed-out nut or just with their hands. Can you whistle using your hands? It's pretty difficult!

?

Humans and animals might not speak the same language, but that doesn't mean they can't communicate – as this impressive partnership shows us.

Honey tastes great, and humans have been eating it for thousands of years. The only problem is that it can be difficult to find, with beehives usually hidden inside tree trunks.

But some people in sub-Saharan Africa have found a way to solve that. Over generations, they've worked out that by making a special call they can summon the greater honeyguide bird, which gets its name from an amazing ability to locate a hive.

The bird then flies from tree to tree, making clicking sounds as it goes to ensure the humans are following, before eventually leading them straight to the prize.

Once the hive has been located, the humans use smoke to clear out the bees (the bit that the birds couldn't do on their own) before carefully removing the honeycomb. The honeyguides then swoop down to feast on the discarded beeswax. What a dream team!

STICK WITH ME, KID

SHARKS AND REMORA FISH

At first glance, a remora seems like a fairly regular fish, but if you look closely you'll see it has a flat head with a tread on top as if it's been run over by the wheel of a car.

It might appear odd, but the tread is actually part of the remora's suction disc and gives the fish the ability to attach itself to something and stay there, no matter what.

Intriguingly, it uses this superpower to attach itself to the scariest fish in the sea: sharks! It does this because sharks are covered in parasitic creatures that the remora fish likes to eat – and the sharks are more than happy for them to be removed because it lessens the chance of them being exposed to harmful bacteria.

The remora fish also uses its suction disc to cling to other creatures, like manta rays, whales and even the occasional scuba diver!

?

The suction disc on a remora is actually the front fin on its back, which has gradually evolved over millions of years to provide the fish with its special sticking power.
 If you had the power to stick to anything, what would you choose?

When the shark goes looking for its own meal, the fish clings on and goes along for the ride. As soon as the predator's caught its prey, the remora detaches itself and hoovers up any leftovers from the messy meal.

Male waterbucks have an impressive set of spiralling horns on their heads, which can grow up to one metre in length and be deployed as an effective weapon in battle.

IGNORE THE SMELL – WE'RE SWELL

WATERBUCKS AND CATTLE EGRETS

Following the oxpecker's lead, cattle egrets in sub-Saharan Africa have found that life can be a lot easier if they're brave enough to make friends with a big beast.

In this relationship, the big beast is a waterbuck – a large antelope that is known for being particularly smelly because it releases a musky odour when it sweats.

Despite the smell, egrets can often be seen close to waterbucks because they like to eat the grasshoppers that leap about when the antelopes disturb them in the long grass.

To thank their four-legged friends, the birds keep an eye out for predators like hyenas and wild dogs and make a loud call if they see any trouble coming their way.

The waterbuck is well named because it's more water-dependent than a lot of Africa's mammals and is always close to a water source. This means that if an egret sounds the alarm, the buck can retreat into a lake or river and show off its super swimming skills.

Waterbucks are easy to identify because they have white markings on their bottoms. This comes in handy when herds are navigating through dense grasslands as it helps the younger antelopes keep sight of the leaders.

THE BIG BEAST SPA

HIPPOS AND BARBEL FISH

Hippos are one of the biggest land mammals in the world – only elephants and rhinos are bigger! – but they actually spend most of their time hanging out in the water.

Their favourite spots to keep cool are shallow lakes and rivers. If you were walking past, you might spot their big heads and little ears poking out.

Despite their size, hippos are really good swimmers, and they can hold their breath underwater for a surprisingly long time. Can you guess how long?
a) a minute
b) 5 minutes
c) 10 minutes

?

What you wouldn't see, though, is the extensive spa treatment they're getting under the water from barbel fish, who like to swarm round their big buddies and gobble up all the parasitic insects that enjoy gorging on the hippos.

This treatment even includes dental care, with the hippo opening its huge mouth – and promising not to snap it shut – while the fish dart in and pick out food between its teeth.

They might sound like a pretty cute couple, but here's the yucky bit. When they're not cleaning the hippos, barbel fish swim closely behind them and wait for a delivery of their favourite snack: hippo poo!

The name 'hippopotamus' comes from the ancient Greek word for 'river horse' – but modern science has found that they're more closely related to whales and dolphins.

ANSWER – b) It's an impressive 5 minutes!

81

OCEANIA

The world's smallest continent, Oceania, consists of Australia, New Zealand and thousands of smaller islands in the Pacific Ocean. On land, some of the most well-known animals are kangaroos, koalas, wombats and kiwis – but surprisingly Australia is also home to the world's largest population of camels. In the waters that surround Oceania's islands, you'll find the Great Barrier Reef, the world's largest coral reef system, and a whole host of incredible sea creatures like whales, sharks, rays and turtles.

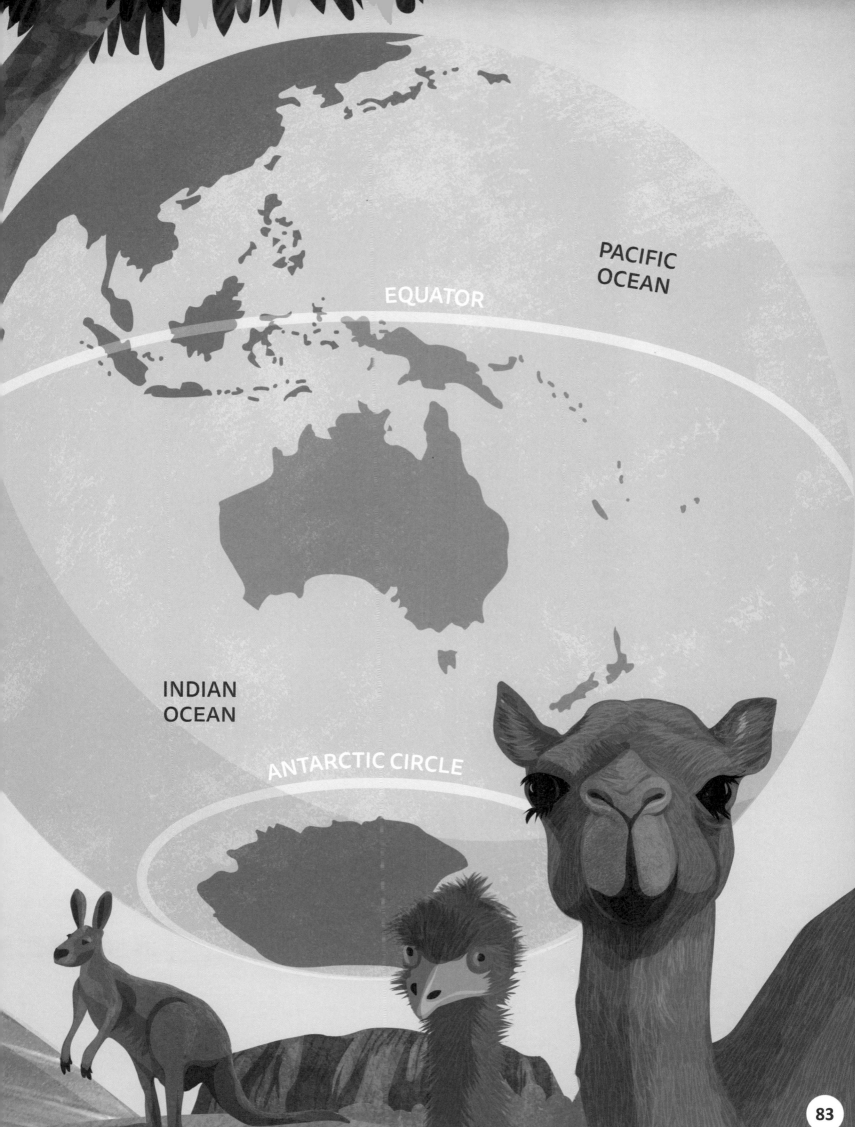

PACIFIC
OCEAN

EQUATOR

INDIAN
OCEAN

ANTARCTIC CIRCLE

A SUPERHERO AND ITS SIDEKICK

GOBY FISH AND PISTOL SHRIMPS

If you come across a pistol shrimp, the first thing you'll notice is that it has an ENORMOUS claw – and that's what gives it an incredible superpower.

When the shrimp snaps the giant claw shut, it produces a shockwave that makes one of the loudest noises in the ocean and stuns any nearby prey.

Every good superhero needs a sidekick, though, and pistol shrimps also happen to be almost completely blind. So they get a little help from the gloomy-looking goby fish, which stays in contact with its pal's long antennae until it spots danger and scurries off to safety with the shrimp close behind.

The goby is rewarded for its role by being allowed to share the shrimp's expertly excavated home beneath the seabed, which is handy as the goby can't dig its own. And its burrow is always spotless because the shrimp also happens to be a brilliant cleaner.

The noise made by snapping shrimps is so loud that it can interfere with military sonar systems, which are used to detect objects in the ocean by bouncing sound waves off them. The shrimps' noise is even thought to have stopped the Japanese from spotting some US submarines during World War Two.

If pistol shrimps lose their mega claw in a battle, a smaller pincer is grown to replace it, and the other one eventually swells to become a new giant stunning snapper.

Ants have been scurrying about since dinosaurs were roaming the Earth, and researchers think they have been helping plants out for tens of millions of years.

ANTS IN YOUR PLANTS

EPIPHYTIC PLANTS AND ANTS

Plants that live on other plants are known as epiphytes, and to survive they have found clever ways to collect and retain water and nutrients so they can grow without soil.

They often get their water from moisture in the air, like rain or mist, but to source the nutrients they need they've developed a partnership with a helpful little insect.

The plants use their strange stems, called rhizomes, to latch on to trees, and these bulbous roots contain a network of tunnels and chambers that offer a great home for ant colonies, who provide a constant supply of nutrient-rich waste.

They also act as the plant's own little army, marching swiftly off to defeat any rival insects who land on the plant and try to have a nibble. So, while neither the plants nor the ants depend on each other to survive, their relationship does make their lives a little easier.

As well as protecting plants, ants also help them by dispersing their seeds and carrying them much further afield than they would otherwise be able to travel.

Mangrove trees help protect the land by reducing the impact of erosion on the coastline but, despite this, they are still at risk from human deforestation.

LIVING ON THE EDGE
MANGROVE FORESTS AND CRABS

Plants usually do their best to avoid saltwater, but that's what makes mangroves so unusual because these resilient trees thrive in areas that are regularly submerged by the sea.

At high tide, the bottoms of these trees are underwater, but when the tide recedes it reveals a web of mangrove roots that helps keep the ocean clean by trapping and filtering sediment, which in turn protects seagrass and corals.

These sheltered forests also provide the perfect place for lots of different animals to find food and reproduce – like lobsters and fish below the water, and birds and bats above it.

One animal that is particularly important to the life of mangrove trees is the crab because it eats the leaves of the tree, which helps recycle the nutrients back into the ecosystem. The burrows they dig also help the trees grow by increasing oxygen levels in the mud.

Mangrove forests can be found on the coasts of over 100 countries around the world, and according to NASA they cover more than 50,000 square miles of the Earth's surface.

A COLOURFUL COMBO

CORAL AND ALGAE

One of the oldest symbiotic relationships in the world is the union between coral and algae, which some scientists think could date back more than 200 million years and is so resilient that it managed to survive the mass extinction event that wiped out the dinosaurs.

Although coral looks like an underwater plant, its structures are made up of lots of cylindrical creatures called coral polyps.

These polyps are translucent, meaning they have colourless bodies that light can pass through, so it's actually the algae that grows on the polyps that gives coral the bright colours it's known for.

Through photosynthesis, the algae is able to produce natural sugars that feed the coral polyps and allow them to grow, and it is given a structure to call home in return.

However, if the coral becomes stressed from pollution or warmer water, it expels the algae and loses its colour in a process known as bleaching. This makes it harder for the coral to survive and is one reason experts fear climate change could put their future at risk.

Coral polyps can come in lots of different sizes, ranging from tiny ones the size of a pin to giant ones as big as a football.

Coral reefs cover less than 1 per cent of the world's ocean floor, but they are home to a much higher percentage of marine life. Can you guess what it is?
a) 5 per cent
b) 10 per cent
c) 25 per cent

?

ANSWER – c! It's thought that coral reefs are home to 25 per cent of all marine life.

When polyps connect to one another, they form a colony that becomes a single living thing, and when lots of these colonies join together they form a coral reef. The largest example of this is the Great Barrier Reef off the coast of Australia.

HOW CAN WE BE FRIENDS OF NATURE?

Well, we've reached the end of our journey round the globe – thanks for coming along! We've learnt about all sorts of incredible symbiotic relationships, from superhero shrimps and their goby sidekicks to the mysterious fungi that helps trees talk to one another.

Do you have a favourite one? Whatever it is, we hope it's helped you understand how our beautiful planet and so much of the life on it depends on co-operation between species.

Sadly, though, humans can be a threat to some of these fragile relationships.

Mangrove forests, for example, are being cut down for firewood and to make way for fish farms and property developments, while the global bee population is declining due to the continued use of harmful pesticides and the destruction of wildflower meadows.

And, of course, there is an increasing risk to a huge number of animals and plants and their habitats from human-induced climate change, which increases the likelihood of extreme weather events like heatwaves, floods, droughts and wildfires.

It's easy to feel sad and overwhelmed about these threats to our wildlife, especially when the

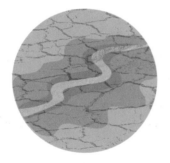  

We've seen that humans can also develop these amazing partnerships, be it with the brilliant bacteria in our bodies or the dolphins that help people catch fish in Brazil. And maybe you can think of some more species that we might be able to join forces with!

power to change them often lies with the leaders of our countries and big corporations. But there are ways we can all make a difference to our local environment, and some of these small things can have a big impact on our planet – like keeping the sea clean so bobtail squids can carry on glowing and sunfish can keep sunbathing.

Here are a few of our suggestions:

Be a bit wild!
Choose a spot in your garden and let the weeds take over. The wildflowers that emerge will help feed bees, butterflies and more.

Get creative!
If you don't have a garden, don't worry – you only need a small space and planting some seeds in a pot on your windowsill will still help.

Go on a beach clean!
Removing litter from our beaches is a brilliant way to help marine animals as everything you bag is one less thing that could endanger them.

Reduce, reuse, recycle!
Cutting the amount of waste we produce also helps stop harmful plastics from ending up in our seas, so try to use fewer disposable things.

Try people power!
Are there journeys you take in a car that you could make on foot or by bike? If so, that's a great way to reduce pollution and make our air cleaner.

If we all try our hardest to respect Earth and all the life on it, hopefully these amazing symbiotic relationships will be around for millions of years to come!